Can These Bones Live?

By
Jemima Love

*This book is dedicated to my children
Brittany, Jasmine, and Markieth.*

I will teach you by the hand of God. Job 27:11

Kizzie sang a song about a man
who raised dry bones by God's command.
"Dry bones?" said Natasha. "I have not heard.
Are you sure this story is in The Word?"

"Oh yes" said Jemima. "This is it here.
Now have a seat and open your ears.
Ezekiel was a prophet who God wanted to show
His awesome power to raise dry bones."

"Can these bones live now that they're dead?
Can these bones live?" His awesome God asked.
"Lord you know so more than I.
If you say yes, then so do I."

God said. "Prophesy to these bones.
Speak into them life,
And watch them rise before your eyes."

**When those bones started rattling and shaking,
Ezekiel's very breath was taken.**

First the bones, then the sinews,
and then the skin begin to renew.
Before my eyes these bones have risen,
And all they needed was breath from heaven.

"Prophesy unto the wind prophesy son of man
Say come from your four ends
and give my children life again."
The wind came rushing to give life,
And they stood alive before my eyes.

God said, "These bones are the house of Israel.
They feel alone, and there hope is miserable.
I am about to make them new.
So I will speak to them through you."

**See my people are so ragged and torn,
all there hope is faded and worn.**

Say this to them so they can know,
"The Father is about to make you whole."
You will be one nation in the land
that sits upon a great mountain."

**Israel shall dwell therein,
their children and their children's children.**

Now Natasha knows the story of the dry bone.
God once again made Israel whole.
She and Kizzy clapped their hands
while singing of dry bones that lived again.

Bible Study

(All verses are copied from the King James Version of the Holy Bible)

Ezekiel 37

¹The hand of the LORD was upon me, and carried me out in the spirit of the LORD, and set me down in the midst of the valley which was full of bones,

²And caused me to pass by them round about: and, behold, there were very many in the open valley; and, lo, they were very dry.

³And he said unto me, Son of man, can these bones live? And I answered, O Lord GOD, thou knowest.

⁴Again he said unto me, Prophesy upon these bones, and say unto them, O ye dry bones, hear the word of the LORD.

⁵Thus saith the Lord GOD unto these bones; Behold, I will cause breath to enter into you, and ye shall live:

⁶And I will lay sinews upon you, and will bring up flesh upon you, and cover you with skin, and put breath in you, and ye shall live; and ye shall know that I am the LORD.

⁷So I prophesied as I was commanded: and as I prophesied, there was a noise, and behold a shaking, and the bones came

together, bone to his bone. ⁸And when I beheld, lo, the sinews and the flesh came up upon them, and the skin covered them above: but there was no breath in them.

⁹Then said he unto me, Prophesy unto the wind, prophesy, son of man, and say to the wind, Thus saith the Lord GOD; Come from the four winds, O breath, and breathe upon these slain, that they may live.

¹⁰So I prophesied as he commanded me, and the breath came into them, and they lived, and stood up upon their feet, an exceeding great army.

[11]Then he said unto me, Son of man, these bones are the whole house of Israel: behold, they say, Our bones are dried, and our hope is lost: we are cut off for our parts.

[12]Therefore prophesy and say unto them, Thus saith the Lord GOD; Behold, O my people, I will open your graves, and cause you to come up out of your graves, and bring you into the land of Israel.

[13]And ye shall know that I am the LORD, when I have opened your graves, O my people, and brought you up out of your graves,

[14]And shall put my spirit in you, and ye shall live, and I shall place you in your own land: then shall ye know that I the LORD have spoken it, and performed it, saith the LORD.

[15]The word of the LORD came again unto me, saying,

[16]Moreover, thou son of man, take thee one stick, and write upon it, For Judah, and for the children of Israel his companions: then take another stick, and write upon it, For Joseph, the stick of Ephraim and for all the house of Israel his companions:

[17]And join them one to another into one stick; and they shall become one in thine hand.

¹⁸And when the children of thy people shall speak unto thee, saying, Wilt thou not shew us what thou meanest by these?

¹⁹Say unto them, Thus saith the Lord GOD; Behold, I will take the stick of Joseph, which is in the hand of Ephraim, and the tribes of Israel his fellows, and will put them with him, even with the stick of Judah, and make them one stick, and they shall be one in mine hand.

²⁰And the sticks whereon thou writest shall be in thine hand before their eyes.

²¹And say unto them, Thus saith the Lord GOD; Behold, I will take the children of Israel from among the heathen, whither they be gone, and will gather them on every side, and bring them into their own land:

²²And I will make them one nation in the land upon the mountains of Israel; and one king shall be king to them all: and they shall be no more two nations, neither shall they be divided into two kingdoms any more at all.

²³Neither shall they defile themselves any more with their idols, nor with their detestable things, nor with any of their transgressions: but I will save them out of all their dwelling

places, wherein they have sinned, and will cleanse them: so shall they be my people, and I will be their God.

²⁴And David my servant shall be king over them; and they all shall have one shepherd: they shall also walk in my judgments, and observe my statutes, and do them.

²⁵And they shall dwell in the land that I have given unto Jacob my servant, wherein your fathers have dwelt; and they shall dwell therein, even they, and their children, and their children's children for ever: and my servant David shall be their prince for ever.

²⁶Moreover I will make a covenant of peace with them; it shall be an everlasting covenant with them: and I will place them, and multiply them, and will set my sanctuary in the midst of them for evermore.

²⁷My tabernacle also shall be with them: yea, I will be their God, and they shall be my people.

²⁸And the heathen shall know that I the LORD do sanctify Israel, when my sanctuary shall be in the midst of them for evermore.